Drawing from the Word

Copyright © 2022 by The Salvation Army USA Southern Territory

All rights reserved. This book or any portion thereof may not be reproduced or used in any manner whatsoever without express written permission of the publisher except for the use of brief quotations in a book review.

For information write:
The Salvation Army
USA Southern Territory
Literary Council
1424 Northeast Expressway
Atlanta, GA 30329

Printed in the United States of America

Scripture taken from the Holy Bible, New International Version®, NIV®. Copyright© 1973, 1978, 1984, 2011 by Biblica, Inc.™ Used by permission of Zondervan. All rights reserved worldwide. www.zondervan.com The "NIV" and "New International Version" are trademarks registered in the United States Patent and Trademark Offices by Biblica, Inc.™

Welcome to a unique way of studying the Book of Esther. I have been inspired to write this because I enjoy journaling and coloring as I reflect on the Scriptures. Using art has been a proven method for retention of information as well as relaxation. This book is designed to be journaled using blank pages for notes, doodles or grand works of art; coloring pages that were inspired by each Bible chapter; and a few prompts to help you to immerse yourself in the story.

The Book of Esther is commonly seen as a book for women to study. In classifying it as a women's only story, we limit the Word of God, a dangerous thing. This book is designed for both women and men alike to grow and create as well as learn from the text. Although the central figure is a woman, the fact that it is included in the Bible tells us that it is there for a reason. There is much we can all learn from Esther.

How to Journal in this book

The journal prompts are designed to enhance the reading and give you the opportunity to put your thoughts into words or pictures as you reflect on the Scripture. This is an opportunity to relax and let your creativity flow!

Suggested materials

Colored pencils work best. If you are new to this medium, I recommend looking up some blending exercises to try on the page provided.

Crayons are a great option for any kind of art journaling. They are vibrant, inexpensive, and easy to use.

Markers are also a good choice for bold colors however, you may experience some bleed through from the back side of the page. This may not bother you. If it does, feel free to prepare your page ahead of time with some gesso. Make sure to put some scrap paper underneath the page you're working on or else you will paint your book shut. Don't ask how I know this.

Paint is not recommended. If you'd like to use paint, I suggest watercolor. My favorite is watercolor pencils because of the control, lack of mess, and versatility. Acrylics are not recommended as they can stick the pages together and add a lot of weight. If you choose paint, I suggest you do so sparingly. Any pages that you plan on painting should be first prepared with a generous layer of gesso.

Oil pastels can be a lot of fun however, if you choose to use pastels, chalks, or charcoals, I recommend sealing the page after you are finished. This can be done using clear packing tape laid across the top. Use long strips and lay them side by side. Then trim the ends once you have everything in place. Another option is a matte Mod Podge painted. Note: Not recommended with marker because it will streak. Make sure to let it dry thoroughly before closing the pages. Tip: gloss Mod Podge will stick your pages together. This happened on one of my favorite spreads I did in my song book. So frustrating!

Any of these items can be found at your local craft store for not much money. I don't suggest any specific brand. Just use what you like or step outside your comfort zone. Use it as an opportunity to try out a fun new medium.

Feel free to try out your chosen medium here.

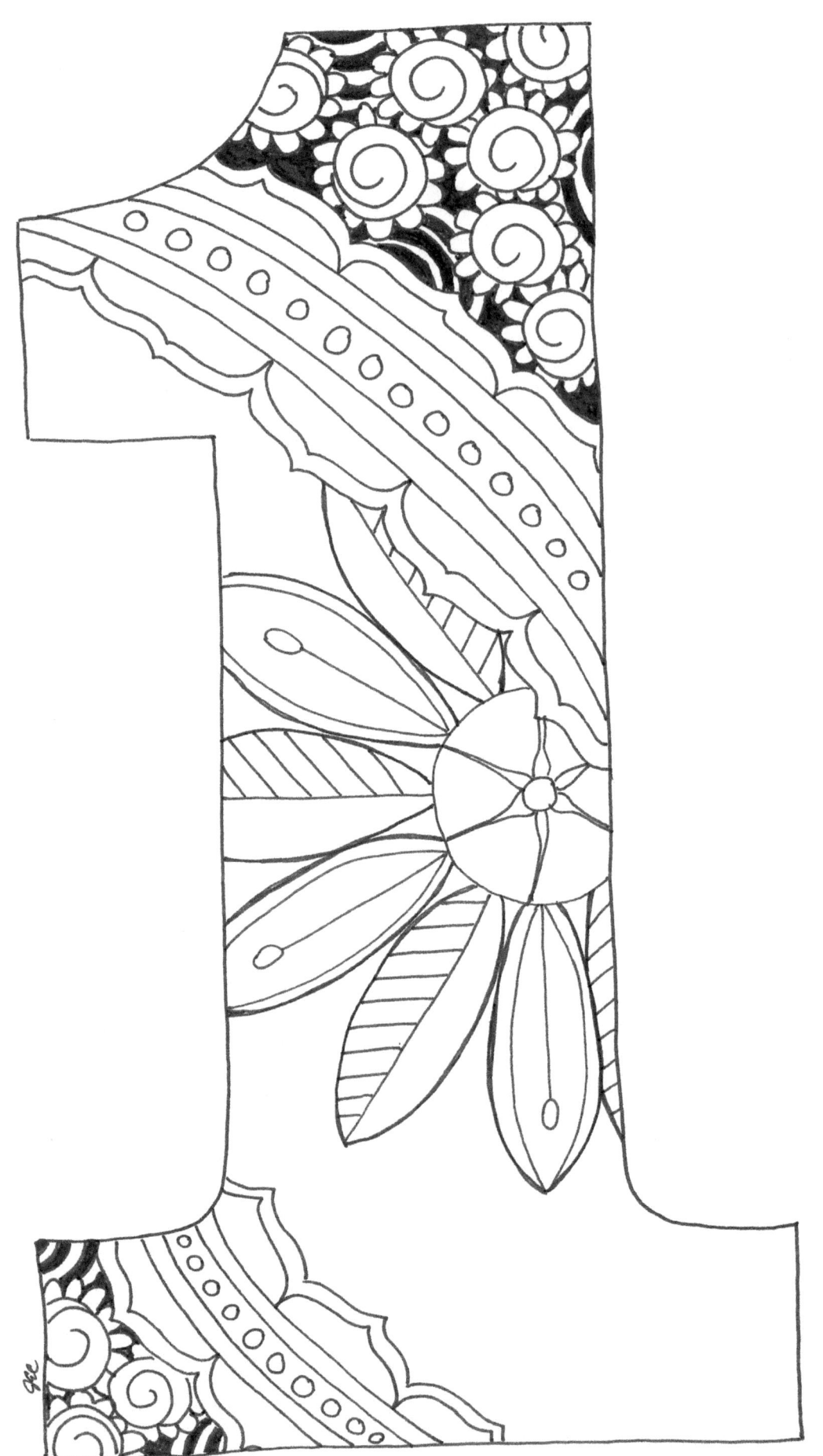

Chapter One

Queen Vashti Deposed

¹ This is what happened during the time of Xerxes, the Xerxes who ruled over 127 provinces stretching from India to Cush: ² At that time King Xerxes reigned from his royal throne in the citadel of Susa, ³ and in the third year of his reign he gave a banquet for all his nobles and officials. The military leaders of Persia and Media, the princes, and the nobles of the provinces were present.

⁴ For a full 180 days he displayed the vast wealth of his kingdom and the splendor and glory of his majesty. ⁵ When these days were over, the king gave a banquet, lasting seven days, in the enclosed garden of the king's palace, for all the people from the least to the greatest who were in the citadel of Susa. ⁶ The garden had hangings of white and blue linen, fastened with cords of white linen and purple material to silver rings on marble pillars. There were couches of gold and silver on a mosaic pavement of porphyry, marble, mother-of-pearl and other costly stones. ⁷ Wine was served in goblets of gold, each one different from the other, and the royal wine was abundant, in keeping with

the king's liberality. ⁸ By the king's command each guest was allowed to drink with no restrictions, for the king instructed all the wine stewards to serve each man what he wished.

⁹ Queen Vashti also gave a banquet for the women in the royal palace of King Xerxes.

¹⁰ On the seventh day, when King Xerxes was in high spirits from wine, he commanded the seven eunuchs who served him — Mehuman, Biztha, Harbona, Bigtha, Abagtha, Zethar and Karkas — ¹¹ to bring before him Queen Vashti, wearing her royal crown, in order to display her beauty to the people and nobles, for she was lovely to look at. ¹² But when the attendants delivered the king's command, Queen Vashti refused to come. Then the king became furious and burned with anger.

¹³ Since it was customary for the king to consult experts in matters of law and justice, he spoke with the wise men who understood the times ¹⁴ and were closest to the king—Karshena, Shethar, Admatha, Tarshish, Meres, Marsena and Memukan, the seven nobles of Persia and Media who had special access to the king and were highest in the kingdom.

¹⁵ "According to law, what must be done to Queen Vashti?" he asked. "She has not obeyed the command of King Xerxes that the eunuchs have taken to her."

¹⁶ Then Memukan replied in the presence of the king and the nobles, "Queen Vashti has done wrong, not only against the king but also against all the nobles and the peoples of all the provinces of King Xerxes. ¹⁷ For the queen's conduct will

become known to all the women, and so they will despise their husbands and say, 'King Xerxes commanded Queen Vashti to be brought before him, but she would not come.' [18] This very day the Persian and Median women of the nobility who have heard about the queen's conduct will respond to all the king's nobles in the same way. There will be no end of disrespect and discord.

[19] "Therefore, if it pleases the king, let him issue a royal decree and let it be written in the laws of Persia and Media, which cannot be repealed, that Vashti is never again to enter the presence of King Xerxes. Also let the king give her royal position to someone else who is better than she. [20] Then when the king's edict is proclaimed throughout all his vast realm, all the women will respect their husbands, from the least to the greatest." [21] The king and his nobles were pleased with this advice, so the king did as Memukan proposed. [22] He sent dispatches to all parts of the kingdom, to each province in its own script and to each people in their own language, proclaiming that every man should be ruler over his own household, using his native tongue.

Comments

In this chapter, we are invited to glimpse life in a Persian palace. King Xerxes has spent months showing off the wealth of his kingdom to visiting dignitaries. What a decadent celebration it must have been. The author describes for us the lavish furnishings they enjoyed. This tells us about the extensive wealth that abounded under Xerxes' rule and their pride in these material things.

It shouldn't really be a surprise that the king treats his wife as a possession. Queen Vashti was put into an awkward situation. What she was asked to do that night could bring dishonor to the king and Persia as well. Many scholars believe that when she was asked to come and show off her beauty, she was summoned to come naked before the men. Vashti was wise enough to understand that entering naked into a room full of drunken men was not a safe proposition for her. She must have been a formidable woman because the text tells us that the king had sent seven eunuchs to retrieve her, but they couldn't get her to budge. She must have put up quite a fight!

Verse 12 says, "But when the attendants delivered the king's command, Queen Vashti refused to come. Then the king became furious and burned with anger."

Out of this anger, Xerxes consulted some of his peers, as was the custom. These are the same men presumably that he's been drinking extensively with. Perhaps they weren't the best choice for giving the king sound advice. The plan that they devise is

Chapter One

to banish Queen Vashti from the king's sight. Essentially, she loses her position and authority. Up to this point, the queen would have served as the authority over the king's harem. This was not a particularly safe place to be. It was full of women who were constantly vying for favor with the king. Their status was directly tied to the offspring they bore, so the more often they were asked into his chambers, the more likely they were to cement their status as a fruitful wife or concubine. Once the king's edict was announced, Vashti was taken from the highest position of respect to the lowest.

This first chapter sets up the history behind Esther's story. In the coming chapters we will see how, although this is a pagan kingdom ruled by a self-centered, wealth obsessed monarch, God's plans for His people prevail. The background of this story seems to present insurmountable circumstances to the Jewish people who were a conquered servant race of the Persians. But none of the circumstances are overwhelming to God. He works through the situation to save His people in an extraordinary way.

What do you think is the key verse in this chapter?

Why do you think the King was so angered by Queen Vashti's refusal to appear before him?

_____
_____
_____
_____
_____
_____
_____
_____

The Queen was put in a very awkward, no-win situation. Have you ever found yourself in similar position? How did you or how should you have reacted?

_____

_____

_____

_____

_____

_____

Like Vashti, it is often hard to see past what is going on now and imagine how God is using our circumstances for His plan. But we can be assured that He is always there and knows what we are facing. Has there been an event in your life that seemed difficult at the time, but looking back you can see how God used it for good?

_____

_____

_____

_____

_____

_____

Chapter One

Take some time to pray and ask God what He is trying to teach you through His word today.

Journal your thoughts below:

_____

_____

_____

_____

_____

_____

_____

_____

_____

_____

_____

_____

_____

_____

_____

_____

_____

Chapter 2

Esther Made Queen

² Later when King Xerxes' fury had subsided, he remembered Vashti and what she had done and what he had decreed about her. ² Then the king's personal attendants proposed, "Let a search be made for beautiful young virgins for the king. ³ Let the king appoint commissioners in every province of his realm to bring all these beautiful young women into the harem at the citadel of Susa. Let them be placed under the care of Hegai, the king's eunuch, who is in charge of the women; and let beauty treatments be given to them. ⁴ Then let the young woman who pleases the king be queen instead of Vashti." This advice appealed to the king, and he followed it.

⁵ Now there was in the citadel of Susa a Jew of the tribe of Benjamin, named Mordecai son of Jair, the son of Shimei, the son of Kish, ⁶ who had been carried into exile from Jerusalem by Nebuchadnezzar king of Babylon, among those taken captive with Jehoiachin king of Judah. ⁷ Mordecai had a cousin named Hadassah, whom he had brought up because she had neither father nor mother. This young woman, who was also known

as Esther, had a lovely figure and was beautiful. Mordecai had taken her as his own daughter when her father and mother died.

⁸ When the king's order and edict had been proclaimed, many young women were brought to the citadel of Susa and put under the care of Hegai. Esther also was taken to the king's palace and entrusted to Hegai, who had charge of the harem. ⁹ She pleased him and won his favor. Immediately he provided her with her beauty treatments and special food. He assigned to her seven female attendants selected from the king's palace and moved her and her attendants into the best place in the harem.

¹⁰ Esther had not revealed her nationality and family background, because Mordecai had forbidden her to do so. ¹¹ Every day he walked back and forth near the courtyard of the harem to find out how Esther was and what was happening to her.

¹² Before a young woman's turn came to go in to King Xerxes, she had to complete twelve months of beauty treatments prescribed for the women, six months with oil of myrrh and six with perfumes and cosmetics. ¹³ And this is how she would go to the king: Anything she wanted was given her to take with her from the harem to the king's palace. ¹⁴ In the evening she would go there and in the morning return to another part of the harem to the care of Shaashgaz, the king's eunuch who was in charge of the concubines. She would not return to the king unless he was pleased with her and summoned her by name.

¹⁵ When the turn came for Esther (the young woman Mordecai had adopted, the daughter of his uncle Abihail) to go to the

king, she asked for nothing other than what Hegai, the king's eunuch who was in charge of the harem, suggested. And Esther won the favor of everyone who saw her. ¹⁶ She was taken to King Xerxes in the royal residence in the tenth month, the month of Tebeth, in the seventh year of his reign.

¹⁷ Now the king was attracted to Esther more than to any of the other women, and she won his favor and approval more than any of the other virgins. So he set a royal crown on her head and made her queen instead of Vashti. ¹⁸ And the king gave a great banquet, Esther's banquet, for all his nobles and officials. He proclaimed a holiday throughout the provinces and distributed gifts with royal liberality.

Mordecai Uncovers a Conspiracy
¹⁹ When the virgins were assembled a second time, Mordecai was sitting at the king's gate. ²⁰ But Esther had kept secret her family background and nationality just as Mordecai had told her to do, for she continued to follow Mordecai's instructions as she had done when he was bringing her up.

²¹ During the time Mordecai was sitting at the king's gate, Bigthana and Teresh, two of the king's officers who guarded the doorway, became angry and conspired to assassinate King Xerxes. ²² But Mordecai found out about the plot and told Queen Esther, who in turn reported it to the king, giving credit to Mordecai. ²³ And when the report was investigated and found to be true, the two officials were impaled on poles. All this was recorded in the book of the annals in the presence of the king.

Drawing from the Word

What is the key verse in Chapter 2?

In this chapter, we see the king getting more advice from some of his advisors. The Scripture doesn't tell us how much time has passed between chapters 1 and 2, but we're given the impression that this is well past the party and that the king has had some time to sober up and recall what happened with Queen Vashti.

King Xerxes followed the advice of his advisors to hold a sort of audition for a new queen. He couldn't take back what he'd done because the word of the king was considered to be infallible. So, even if he regretted his ill-advised drunken decision, he couldn't change his mind. But when the idea to replace her was presented, the Scripture tells us that this appealed to him.

We've often romanticized this portion of Scripture and compared it to a beauty contest or even a season of *The Bachelor*. But this is far from what actually happened. The main difference is that these women didn't have a choice. They didn't sign up for this and the king was allowed to do with them whatever he pleased while they were in his harem. Those who were not chosen were sent to the chamber with the concubines to wait for when the king once again desired their company. This is a far cry from the fantasy of a rose ceremony!

Esther must have been intelligent as well as beautiful and charming. Unlike the king, she chose her advisors very wisely. Her cousin, and father figure, Mordecai told her to keep her true identity a secret. The Jewish people were a race under the rule of the Persians at the time of this book. They were considered less than the Persians. Had Esther chosen to defy this suggestion, she probably wouldn't have even been considered for the position. Instead, she might have been forced into a lowly position in the palace or elsewhere in the kingdom. But she listened to the advice of Hegai, the eunuch. By following his counsel, she went to the king and gained his favor.

We can definitely see God's hand at work in Esther's life. He brought people into her life that gave her good advice that helped her become the queen.

Even though she was in a dangerous situation, God was in control, placing His people within the palace of an oppressive, pagan country in order to rescue them. Mordechai overheard the plot to murder king Xerxes. Instead of seeing it as an opportunity to join the coup and overthrow the current rulers, he chose to do the right thing. He informed Esther and she took the news to the king. The plotters were punished. Strangely, Mordecai's interception was for a time forgotten.

Chapter Two

All these events are crucial to the rest of the story. They weren't aware of what God had in store, but they were faithful and trusted Him to work out His good plan for His people.

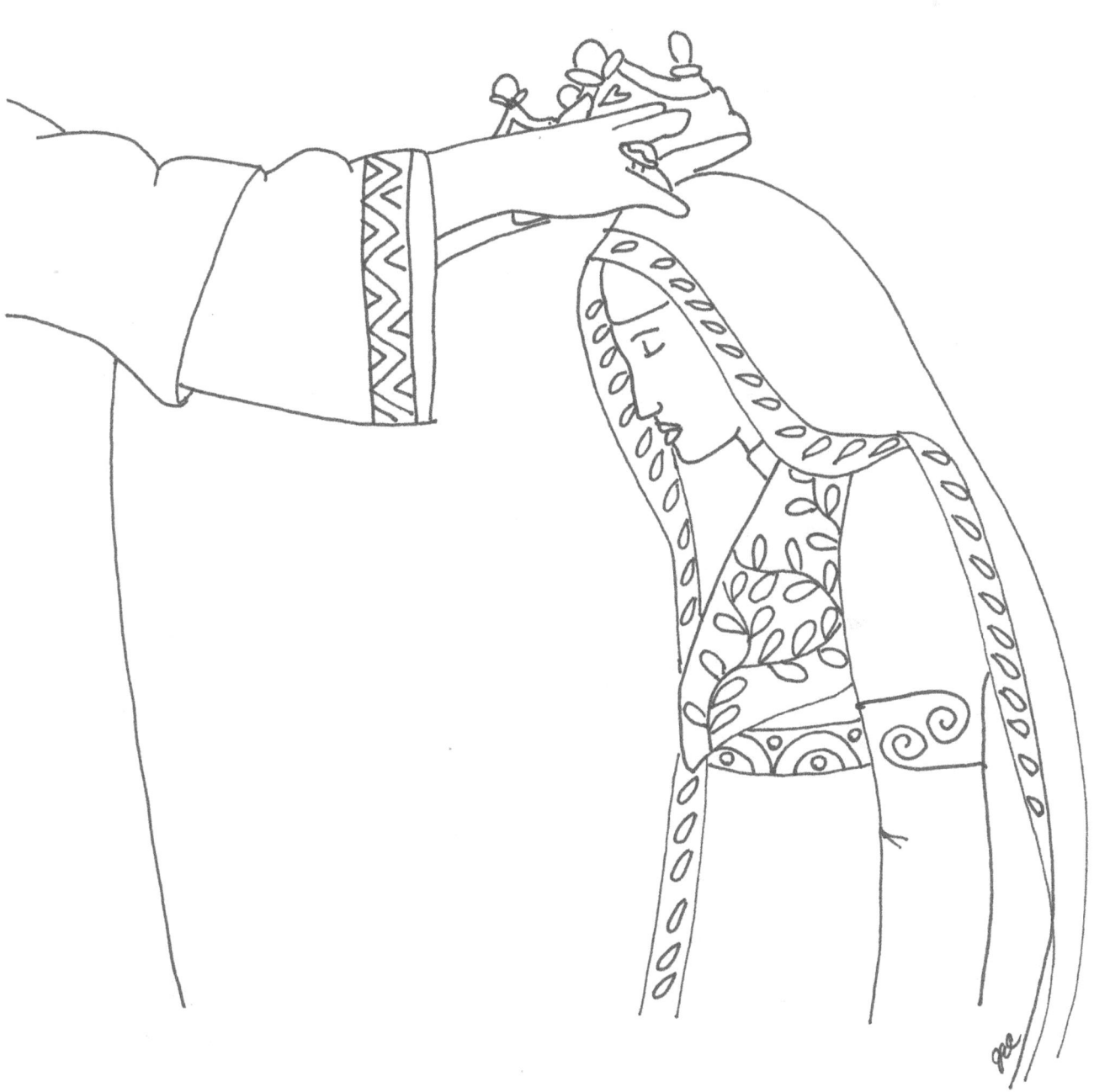

In this chapter, Esther hid her identity. Have you ever been in a situation where you felt you couldn't be yourself?

_____

_____

_____

_____

_____

_____

_____

_____

How has taking advice from others impacted your decisions? Do you ever regret listening to a one voice over another?

_____

_____

_____

_____

_____

_____

_____

Chapter Two

Was there a time you can look back on in your life where perhaps it was confusing, but now you can see that God was at work?

_____
_____
_____
_____
_____
_____
_____

Are you currently facing a struggle or know someone who is that seems overwhelming?

_____
_____
_____
_____
_____
_____
_____
_____

Do you have someone that looks out for you like Mordecai looked out for Esther?

_____

_____

_____

_____

_____

_____

_____

_____

_____

_____

God cares for us each and watches over us just as Mordecai watched over Esther.

Take some time to thank God for those He has placed in your life who have looked out for you. Thank Him for how far you've come and release the anxiety you are currently experiencing. Although we don't always understand, we can trust that He is in control of all the situations we face. God is concerned with both the big picture as well as the individual one.

Chapter Two

Take some time to journal your feelings here.

_____

_____

_____

_____

_____

_____

_____

_____

_____

_____

_____

_____

_____

_____

_____

_____

Chapter 3

Haman's Plot to Destroy the Jews

3 After these events, King Xerxes honored Haman son of Hammedatha, the Agagite, elevating him and giving him a seat of honor higher than that of all the other nobles. 2 All the royal officials at the king's gate knelt down and paid honor to Haman, for the king had commanded this concerning him. But Mordecai would not kneel down or pay him honor.

3 Then the royal officials at the king's gate asked Mordecai, "Why do you disobey the king's command?" 4 Day after day they spoke to him but he refused to comply. Therefore they told Haman about it to see whether Mordecai's behavior would be tolerated, for he had told them he was a Jew.

5 When Haman saw that Mordecai would not kneel down or pay him honor, he was enraged. 6 Yet having learned who Mordecai's people were, he scorned the idea of killing only Mordecai. Instead Haman looked for a way to destroy all Mordecai's people, the Jews, throughout the whole kingdom of Xerxes.

7 In the twelfth year of King Xerxes, in the first month, the month of Nisan, the *pur* (that is, the lot) was cast in the presence of Haman to select a day and month. And the lot fell on the

twelfth month, the month of Adar.

⁸ Then Haman said to King Xerxes, "There is a certain people dispersed among the peoples in all the provinces of your kingdom who keep themselves separate. Their customs are different from those of all other people, and they do not obey the king's laws; it is not in the king's best interest to tolerate them. ⁹ If it pleases the king, let a decree be issued to destroy them, and I will give ten thousand talents of silver to the king's administrators for the royal treasury."

¹⁰ So the king took his signet ring from his finger and gave it to Haman son of Hammedatha, the Agagite, the enemy of the Jews. ¹¹ "Keep the money," the king said to Haman, "and do with the people as you please."

¹² Then on the thirteenth day of the first month the royal secretaries were summoned. They wrote out in the script of each province and in the language of each people all Haman's orders to the king's satraps, the governors of the various provinces and the nobles of the various peoples. These were written in the name of King Xerxes himself and sealed with his own ring. ¹³ Dispatches were sent by couriers to all the king's provinces with the order to destroy, kill and annihilate all the Jews—young and old, women and children—on a single day, the thirteenth day of the twelfth month, the month of Adar, and to plunder their goods. ¹⁴ A copy of the text of the edict was to be issued as law in every province and made known to the people of every nationality so they would be ready for that day.

¹⁵ The couriers went out, spurred on by the king's command, and the edict was issued in the citadel of Susa. The king and Haman sat down to drink, but the city of Susa was bewildered.

What is the key verse in this chapter?

In Chapter 3 we begin understanding who Haman really is. When the king was angry, he deposed Queen Vashti taking his wrath out only on her. But when Haman's temper flares, not only does he seek revenge on Mordecai for his insolence, but decides to kill all the Jewish people.

Like many biblical heroes, Mordecai understanding the risk, chose not to bow before an ungodly authority. His fellow guards asked him over and again what he's doing, but he refused to answer them. Haman, an Agagite, belonged to one of the historic enemies of the Jews called the Amorites. This no doubt explains the animosity between the men. Mordecai's defiance completely enraged Haman.

It doesn't seem to take much to set Haman off. He had people all over the country bowing to him and one that didn't. He focused on that one, letting his anger consume him. It's easy to let the one or two bad things that happen to us ruin an otherwise good day. But Haman's response far exceeded any insult he perceived from Mordecai. Genocide was an extreme way to retaliate.

In verse 7 we see them casting lots. It is assumed that Haman would have consulted the court astrologers for this. It was common practice at the time for officials to cast lots to determine days that would be predicted to be lucky for the year. These days would then be set aside for important events.

This part of the story serves as a critical portion of the plot as well as a way to hightlight the gap between the Persian and Jewish cultures. The Persian Empire was a pagan culture that relied on divinations and astrology. This is in direct contrast to the Jewish people who worshipped only God and took their direction from Him. While it is true that the casting of lots appears in other books of the Bible, such as in Acts when a new disciple needed to be chosen, they did so to seek the supreme authority of God's will. The story of Esther doesn't end with the "happily ever after" tagline, but her rise to the palace is only the beginning of a much greater story.

Chapter three shows us a little more about the culture that the Persians had forced onto the Jewish people when they were under their rule. Is this relatable at all? Have you ever found yourself in a situation where you felt powerless and didn't agree with those who had authority over you?

_____

_____

_____

_____

_____

_____

_____

While we generally would much rather relate to Esther or Mordechai, put yourself in Haman's shoes for a moment. What do you feel was the true driving force behind his anger?

_____

_____

_____

_____

_____

_____

_____

Chapter Three

Facing dangerous situations is a common theme in the book of Esther. Is there a situation that you have been avoiding that may need to be faced? Pray about it. That God's will prevail and that He will make good out of whatever comes.

Please journal your thoughts here

_____
_____
_____
_____
_____
_____
_____
_____
_____
_____
_____
_____
_____
_____

Chapter four

Mordecai Persuades Esther to Help

4 When Mordecai learned of all that had been done, he tore his clothes, put on sackcloth and ashes, and went out into the city, wailing loudly and bitterly. 2 But he went only as far as the king's gate, because no one clothed in sackcloth was allowed to enter it. 3 In every province to which the edict and order of the king came, there was great mourning among the Jews, with fasting, weeping and wailing. Many lay in sackcloth and ashes.

4 When Esther's eunuchs and female attendants came and told her about Mordecai, she was in great distress. She sent clothes for him to put on instead of his sackcloth, but he would not accept them. 5 Then Esther summoned Hathak, one of the king's eunuchs assigned to attend her, and ordered him to find out what was troubling Mordecai and why.

6 So Hathak went out to Mordecai in the open square of the city in front of the king's gate. 7 Mordecai told him everything that had happened to him, including the exact amount of money Haman had promised to pay into the royal treasury for the destruction of the Jews. 8 He also gave him a copy of the text of the edict for their annihilation, which had been published in Susa, to show to Esther and explain it to her, and he told him to instruct her to go into the king's presence to beg for mercy and plead with him for her people.

9 Hathak went back and reported to Esther what Mordecai had said. 10 Then she instructed him to say to Mordecai, 11 "All the king's officials and the people of the royal provinces know that

for any man or woman who approaches the king in the inner court without being summoned the king has but one law: that they be put to death unless the king extends the gold scepter to them and spares their lives. But thirty days have passed since I was called to go to the king."

[12] When Esther's words were reported to Mordecai, [13] he sent back this answer: "Do not think that because you are in the king's house you alone of all the Jews will escape. [14] For if you remain silent at this time, relief and deliverance for the Jews will arise from another place, but you and your father's family will perish. And who knows but that you have come to your royal position for such a time as this?"

Chapter Four

¹⁵ Then Esther sent this reply to Mordecai: ¹⁶ "Go, gather together all the Jews who are in Susa, and fast for me. Do not eat or drink for three days, night or day. I and my attendants will fast as you do. When this is done, I will go to the king, even though it is against the law. And if I perish, I perish."

¹⁷ So Mordecai went away and carried out all of Esther's instructions.

What do you think is the key verse in this chapter?

News had gotten out about Haman's plan to destroy Mordecai and his people. Esther was in a unique position as the new queen of Persia and her cousin was aware of the potential power she possessed. He went before the gates and met with her servants to explain the situation.

Esther's response might seem a little odd. At first, she doesn't show any concern for the destruction of the Jewish people, but rather, concern for herself. Perhaps she was hoping that there was another way, a petition, or maybe a priest could request an audience. Someone else with some experience and authority. Esther was just a pretty girl that caught the king's fancy. She was already way outside her comfort zone.

Esther, and possibly others, may have only seen her as a naïve, lucky girl, but Mordecai reminded her that she was so much more.

We are reminded of Moses when he pleaded with God to send someone else. He knew that there must have been someone more capable than him. But God knew that he was the man for the job, just as Esther was the woman for this one.

We often feel insignificant when faced with God's plan for our lives. Can you imagine how overwhelming the "big picture" must be? When opportunities arise to stand up for God's people and answer His call, it might be tempting to say to yourself, "Someone else should do it." But if we can learn anything from Esther it's that God uses the average, weak, and/or insignificant to take His message where He needs it - if only we are brave enough to take on the challenge.

Read these verses and journal what you think God is saying to you today.

Perhaps this is the moment for which you were created. (Esther 4:14)

"My grace is sufficient for you, My power is made perfect in weakness" (2 Corinthians 12:9).

"Be strong and courageous. Do not fear or be in dread of them, for it is the Lord your God who goes with you. He will not leave you or forsake you" (Deuteronomy 31:6).

"Have I not commanded you? Be strong and courageous. Do not be afraid; do not be discouraged, for the LORD your God will be with you wherever you go" (Joshua 1:9)

Stop. Pause to pray for whatever burdens are currently on your heart.

Drawing from the Word

Use these pages to journal your thoughts

Chapter four

Chapter Five

Esther's Request to the King

⁵ On the third day Esther put on her royal robes and stood in the inner court of the palace, in front of the king's hall. The king was sitting on his royal throne in the hall, facing the entrance. ² When he saw Queen Esther standing in the court, he was pleased with her and held out to her the gold scepter that was in his hand. So Esther approached and touched the tip of the scepter.

³ Then the king asked, "What is it, Queen Esther? What is your request? Even up to half the kingdom, it will be given you."

⁴ "If it pleases the king," replied Esther, "let the king, together with Haman, come today to a banquet I have prepared for him."

⁵ "Bring Haman at once," the king said, "so that we may do what Esther asks."

So the king and Haman went to the banquet Esther had prepared. ⁶ As they were drinking wine, the king again asked Esther, "Now what is your petition? It will be given you. And what is your request? Even up to half the kingdom, it will be granted."

⁷ Esther replied, "My petition and my request is this: ⁸ If the king regards me with favor and if it pleases the king to grant my petition and fulfill my request, let the king and Haman come tomorrow to the banquet I will prepare for them. Then I will answer the king's question."

Haman's Rage Against Mordecai
⁹ Haman went out that day happy and in high spirits. But when he saw Mordecai at the king's gate and observed that he neither rose nor showed fear in his presence, he was filled with rage against Mordecai. ¹⁰ Nevertheless, Haman restrained himself and went home.

Calling together his friends and Zeresh, his wife, ¹¹ Haman boasted to them about his vast wealth, his many sons, and all the ways the king had honored him and how he had elevated him above the other nobles and officials. ¹² "And that's not all," Haman added. "I'm the only person Queen Esther invited to accompany the king to the banquet she gave. And she has invited me along with the king tomorrow. ¹³ But all this gives me no satisfaction as long as I see that Jew Mordecai sitting at the king's gate."

¹⁴ His wife Zeresh and all his friends said to him, "Have a pole set up, reaching to a height of fifty cubits,[a] and ask the king in the morning to have Mordecai impaled on it. Then go with the king to the banquet and enjoy yourself." This suggestion delighted Haman, and he had the pole set up.

Chapter Five

What do you think is the key verse in this chapter?

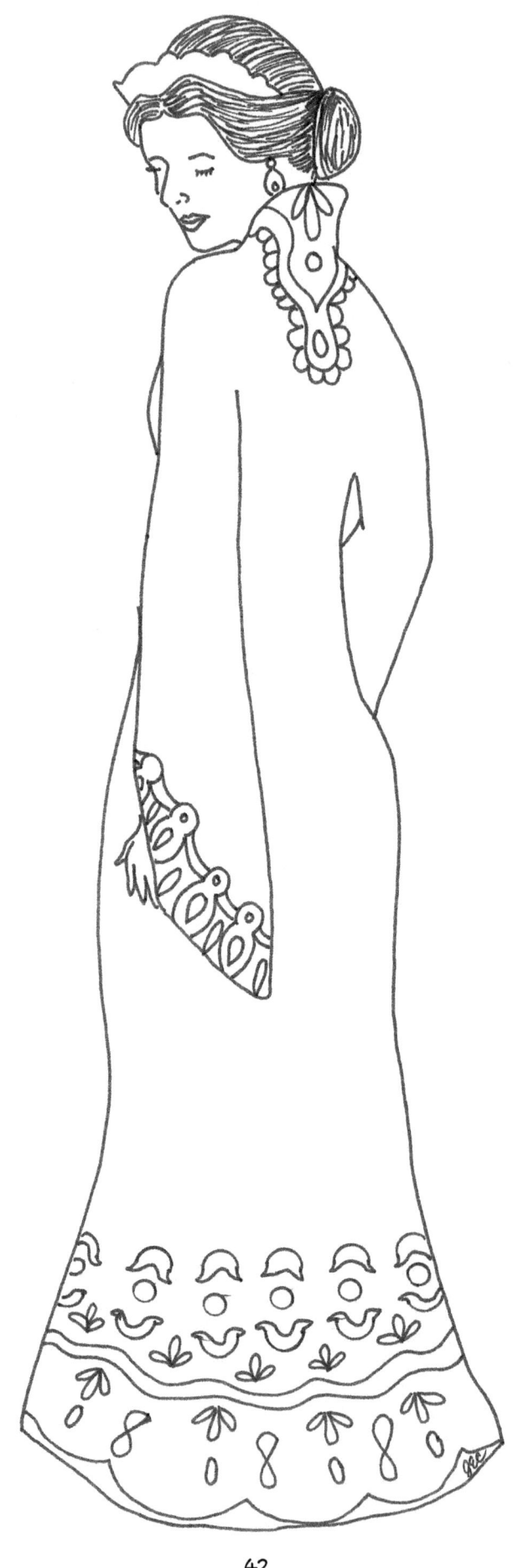

Chapter Five

In chapter five we see a huge contrast between the characters. On one end of the spectrum is the moody, irrational king who promised Esther anything she wanted before even hearing her request. His whims seem to be flowing in her favor in this chapter but the Scripture doesn't tell us why. Then we see the jealous and power hungry Haman described as "happy and in high spirits" in the King James Version he is described as "joyful and pleased of heart," but that doesn't take long to change at all. As soon as he left the palace and saw brave Mordecai, he became enraged at the mere sight of him. It's an interesting reaction. A modern day psychologist could have a field day with this passage. He went to his wife and friends to brag about how great he was. But just seeing his enemy not cowering had bruised his ego so much that he had to run to his cronies and get a refill. Wow! Talk about a narcissist! They help him devise a plan to not only kill Mordecai, but to publicly humiliate him at the same time. Such a death would be spectacle and would draw crowds and much as it is in today's world. The court of public opinion can be harsh and irrational. They would see this man being mocked and jeered and most likely join in. This helped to soothe Haman's bad mood indeed!

Look at the other characterization here. Esther, who was frightened to go before the king, could have taken him at his word and seized the opportunity he offered her to be granted anything, even up to half of his vast kingdom. She knew him by now so instead of blurting out her concerns she made a small, humble request. When she invited the king and his vengeful advisor to her chambers for a banquet, she knew that they would be flattered. She seems well aware of their overinflated egos by this point of the story. Once they were in a more intimate space, perhaps they would let their guards down. In public they did a lot of posturing, and in Haman's case in private too. By asking them to a dinner party in their honor, she is showed wisdom and maturity in stark contrast to the others so far.

We aren't old specifically where she got the inspiration for her plan. However, we have seen how God has surrounded her with sound advisors: Her cousin Mordecai, who raised her and appealed to her loyalty for her people. And we can't forget the counsel she received from Hegai, who helped her through the initial competition for the role as queen. This was not a simple case of good luck. God was definitely looking out for her, and she made sure to pay attention. Doubtless there were other voices in her world that were louder maybe, or even more exciting. The palace was a lively place, full of excitement and intrigue. Despite how interesting the others may have been, Esther chose her friends and advisors wisely. This is a powerful lesson we can take away from this entire book.

It's very easy to get caught up in the drama, poltics and gossip, but at the end of the day the only voice that matters is that of the One who created us. We are reminded that He cares for us and has our best interests in mind. " No temptation has overtaken you except what is common to mankind. And God is faithful; He will not let you be tempted beyond what you can bear. But when you are tempted, He will also provide a way out so that you can endure it" (1 Corinthians 10:13).

We can trust Him no matter the circumstances, even when there are louder voices vying for our attention. We are reminded of the story from 1Kings 19, when Elijah was absolutely distraught, explaining to God that he failed and would rather be dead. From his point of view, everything had gone wrong. It seemed thathe was the only person left that still believed in God, doomed to be murdered by his enemies. God told him to go to the mountain where He was going to pass by. First, there was a tremendous amount of wind that tore the mountain apart. Then an earthquake, followed by a raging fire. But none of these incredible occurrences contained the presence of God. Instead, He spoke to His prophet with the voice of a whisper. In the King James Version, "a still small voice."

It is much easier to follow the crowd pay attention to the flashy and thrilling things that are happening in the world. But if we turn our hearts to hear His whisper, we are getting the best advice from the closest friend we will ever know. reminds us, "Do not be deceived: 'Bad company ruins good morals'" (1 Corinthians 15:33 ESV).

There is an old saying, "you are known by the company you keep." What do you think your current circle of friends says about you?

_____

_____

_____

_____

_____

_____

If you are being truly honest with yourself, do you tend to gravitate towards the wrong kinds of friends? Maybe ones who will only tell you what you want to hear?

_____
_____
_____
_____
_____
_____
_____

Do you have someone you know that you can go to like Mordecai for honest, sound council? Someone who won't just flatter you and bolster your ego?

_____
_____
_____
_____
_____
_____
_____

Chapter Five

Is there something that you need or have needed to share with a friend, but chose to play it safe and encourage them instead?

_____

_____

_____

_____

_____

_____

_____

_____

_____

_____

_____

_____

_____

_____

Take some time to pray for your friends, to ask God to send you (or continue to send you) wise counselors and seek wisdom for any situation in which you could be a better friend to them.

Feel free to journal your thoughts on Chapter Five here

Chapter Five

Chapter Six

Mordecai Honored

⁶ That night the king could not sleep; so he ordered the book of the chronicles, the record of his reign, to be brought in and read to him. ² It was found recorded there that Mordecai had exposed Bigthana and Teresh, two of the king's officers who guarded the doorway, who had conspired to assassinate King Xerxes.

³ "What honor and recognition has Mordecai received for this?" the king asked.

"Nothing has been done for him," his attendants answered.

⁴ The king said, "Who is in the court?" Now Haman had just entered the outer court of the palace to speak to the king about impaling Mordecai on the pole he had set up for him.

⁵ His attendants answered, "Haman is standing in the court."

"Bring him in," the king ordered.

⁶ When Haman entered, the king asked him, "What should be done for the man the king delights to honor?"

Now Haman thought to himself, "Who is there that the king would rather honor than me?" ⁷ So he answered the king, "For the man the king delights to honor, ⁸ have them bring a royal robe the king has worn and a horse the king has ridden, one with a royal crest placed on its head. ⁹ Then let the robe and horse be entrusted to one of the king's most noble princes. Let them robe the man the king delights to honor, and lead him on the horse through the city streets, proclaiming before him, 'This is what is done for the man the king delights to honor!'"

¹⁰ "Go at once," the king commanded Haman. "Get the robe and the horse and do just as you have suggested for Mordecai the Jew, who sits at the king's gate. Do not neglect anything you have recommended."

¹¹ So Haman got the robe and the horse. He robed Mordecai, and led him on horseback through the city streets, proclaiming before him, "This is what is done for the man the king delights to honor!"

¹² Afterward Mordecai returned to the king's gate. But Haman rushed home, with his head covered in grief, ¹³ and told Zeresh his wife and all his friends everything that had happened to him.

His advisers and his wife Zeresh said to him, "Since Mordecai, before whom your downfall has started, is of Jewish origin, you cannot stand against him—you will surely come to ruin!" ¹⁴ While they were still talking with him, the king's eunuchs arrived and hurried Haman away to the banquet Esther had prepared.

Chapter Six

What is the key verse in this chapter?

This chapter seems to start out the same as the others, with King Xerxes and the evil Haman sharing an experience. Neither can sleep. The king called for a scroll of his own great deeds to lull him to sleep. Picture Haman shaking with anticipation for the plot he has hatched. Maybe he was pacing the great hall waiting for the hour the king arrived, practicing his speech or even daydreaming about the congratulatory remarks headed his way. He'd just gotten his ego bolstered by his wife and friends and been the only other guest invited to Esther's dinner party. He was eager to present his latest plan to his buddy, the king. It seemed as if this was going to be a very good day for him, especially when the king brought up the idea of honoring someone for their loyalty. Does this backfire on him! He thought yesterday was a bad day. Just wait Haman. It's about to get way worse.

Imagine his jaw hitting the floor cartoon-style when the king approved the horse, cloak, crown and processional for not Haman, but Mordecai. Not only that, but it is Haman himself who was instructed to parade him through the streets. It had to have bruised his very large and very delicate ego! He ran home with his head covered in shame.

Haman finally got some good advice from his cohorts in verse 13. They tell him to let this one go, that this grudge he has against Mordecai will destroy him. He had to pull himself together for the second banquet of Queen Esther.

This all seems like the plot of a sitcom at times, but we can see God's hand at work here. Had the king been able to sleep that night, he never would have called for his scroll of achievements to be read and wouldn't' have realized Mordecai's unrecognized heroism. God knew of Haman's plan and very creatively dealt with Haman. Here is when we start to see the stories of the king and Haman diverge a bit. One sleepless night seems to change a lot of things.

Did word reached Esther about the recognition of Mordecai? The humiliation of Haman? Perhaps it was this good news that gave her the confidence we see in the next chapter.

Chapter Six

Is there something that you have allowed to steal your joy?

_____

_____

_____

_____

_____

_____

_____

Are you ready to let that go?

_____

_____

_____

_____

_____

_____

_____

If you are being 100% honest, can relate to either the king or to Haman in this story?

_____

_____

Think of a time when you may have been prone to react the way they have in this story.

_____

_____

_____

_____

_____

What do you wish you could have done differently?

_____

_____

_____

_____

_____

Chapter Six

Name a few ways you could avoid repeating this same behavior in the future

_____

_____

_____

_____

_____

_____

_____

The problem occurs, like in our text, that when we allow one thing to get to us and rob us of our joy, it can begin to fester and grow until it eventually becomes hate. When Haman's wife and advisors said that he cannot stand against Mordecai because of his Jewish heritage, they were acknowledging the power of Mordecai's God.

Just as God worked through a sleepless night to save Mordecai, He wants to save us as well. Take a few moments to release whatever it is that has been standing in the way of your joy. Or if nothing comes to mind, ask God to reveal a place in your life that you can improve and experience more of Him.

Drawing from the Word

Please journal your thoughts here

Chapter Six

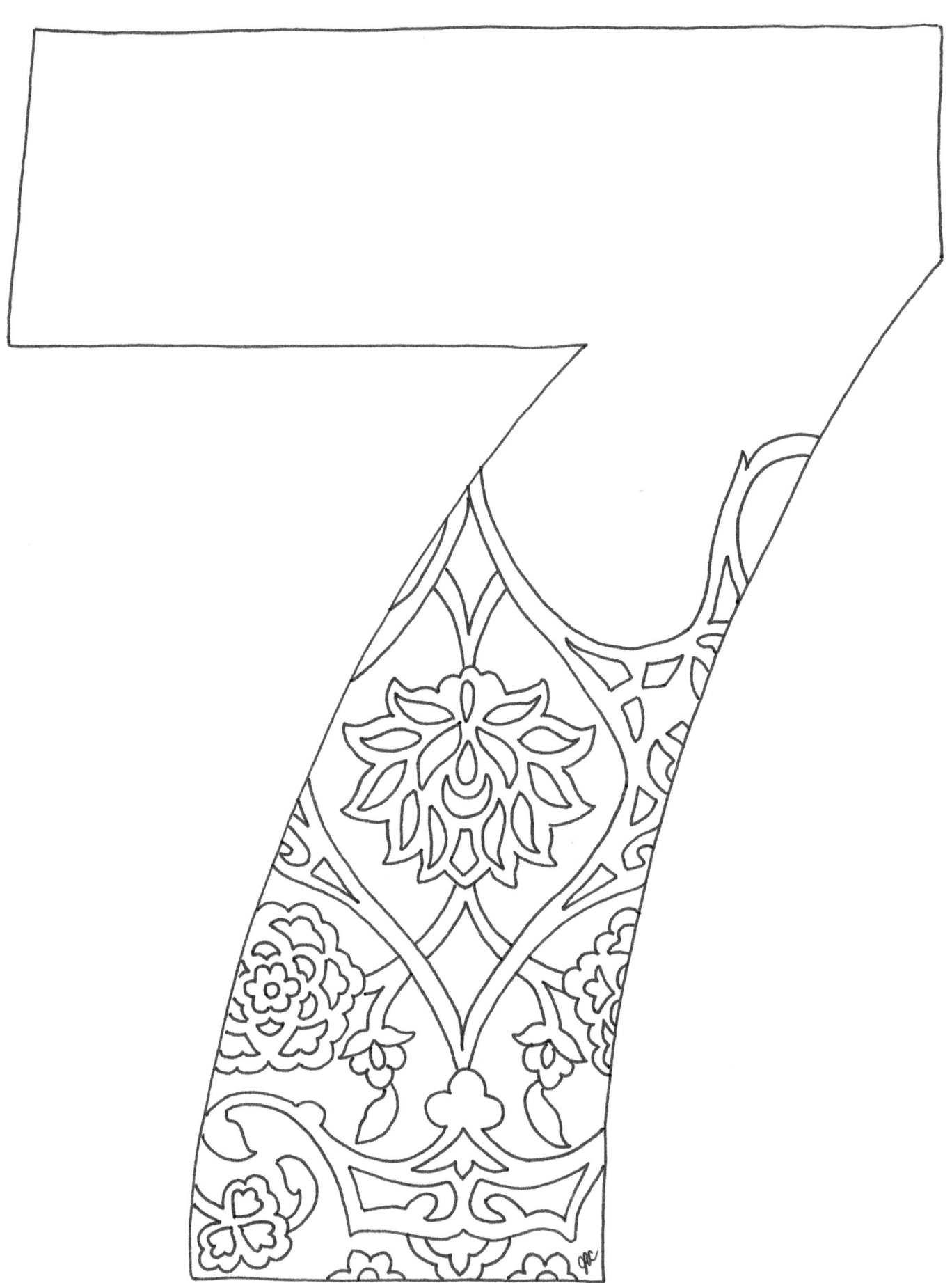

Chapter Seven

Haman Impaled

7 So the king and Haman went to Queen Esther's banquet, 2 and as they were drinking wine on the second day, the king again asked, "Queen Esther, what is your petition? It will be given you. What is your request? Even up to half the kingdom, it will be granted."

3 Then Queen Esther answered, "If I have found favor with you, Your Majesty, and if it pleases you, grant me my life—this is my petition. And spare my people—this is my request. 4 For I and my people have been sold to be destroyed, killed and annihilated. If we had merely been sold as male and female slaves, I would have kept quiet, because no such distress would justify disturbing the king."

5 King Xerxes asked Queen Esther, "Who is he? Where is he—the man who has dared to do such a thing?"

6 Esther said, "An adversary and enemy! This vile Haman!"

Then Haman was terrified before the king and queen. 7 The king got up in a rage, left his wine and went out into the palace garden. But Haman, realizing that the king had already decided his fate, stayed behind to beg Queen Esther for his life.

8 Just as the king returned from the palace garden to the banquet hall, Haman was falling on the couch where Esther was reclining.

The king exclaimed, "Will he even molest the queen while she is with me in the house?"

Drawing from the Word

As soon as the word left the king's mouth, they covered Haman's face. ⁹ Then Harbona, one of the eunuchs attending the king, said, "A pole reaching to a height of fifty cubits stands by Haman's house. He had it set up for Mordecai, who spoke up to help the king."

The king said, "Impale him on it!" ¹⁰ So they impaled Haman on the pole he had set up for Mordecai. Then the king's fury subsided.

What is the key verse in this section?

Esther showed herself to be incredibly brave in this chapter. After throwing her second banquet, she explained to her husband what was going on. We hear him repeat the offer that he has been making to her throughout these past few chapters, "I'll give you whatever you want even up to half of my kingdom."

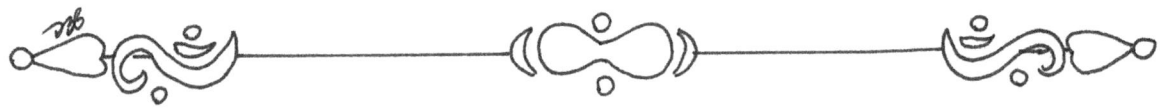

Chapter Seven

He must have known that she wanted a favor from him and not just to make him a fancy dinner. This is the third time in the book that he makes this promise to her and she certainly seized the opportunity.

Queen Esther not only petitioned for her life and the life of her people, she did so tactfully. She doesn't reveal her ethnicity right away but chose her words carefully. The king was outraged that someone would be so bold as to threaten his wife and her people. True to his impulsive nature, his first reaction was to point fingers and punish the guilty party. Esther courageously accused Haman to his face. We can only imagine his reaction. He was probably still off balance from the humiliating day he'd just experienced as he paraded through town and extolled the merits of his sworn enemy. He probably expected this dinner to be just like the one the night before and then-BLAMO! His whole world shattered in an instant.

Mordecai had been wise in choosing his niece as his ally. Her faithfulness to God and His people ultimately saved them all.

Have you wondered if Queen Esther was full of doubt? After all, she may have been queen in title, but she wasn't raised in that lifestyle and culture. In many ways she was still the young Hadassah, who had known great loss and sadness and had to rely on her cousin to live. Her situation may have changed but she didn't let it change who she was. Although, up to this point, she had kept her identity a secret, she didn't forget who she was and where she was from. She may have doubted her worth and abilities against such great odds, but she didn't doubt herself as a child of God. She may even have questioned His decision to use her in such a magnificent way, but she didn't doubt that He could save them.

Do you ever feel like you are in over your head?

___

What sort of doubts run through your mind?

___

A friend once told me that his burdens felt like someone was piling wet blankets on him. They started out not too heavy but as they added up it was stifling. Can you relate to this? Describe what it feels like when you are overwhelmed

___

Chapter Seven

What is your normal reaction when you feel that circumstances are beyond your control?

_____

_____

_____

_____

_____

_____

As a child of God how should we react in these situations?

_____

_____

_____

_____

_____

_____

_____

_____

Take some time to stop and reflect then pray for the courage and wisdom to be who you need to be regardless of the circumstances.

Drawing from the Word

Journal your thoughts here

Chapter Seven

Chapter 8

The King's Edict on Behalf of the Jews

⁸ That same day King Xerxes gave Queen Esther the estate of Haman, the enemy of the Jews. And Mordecai came into the presence of the king, for Esther had told how he was related to her. ² The king took off his signet ring, which he had reclaimed from Haman, and presented it to Mordecai. And Esther appointed him over Haman's estate.

³ Esther again pleaded with the king, falling at his feet and weeping. She begged him to put an end to the evil plan of Haman the Agagite, which he had devised against the Jews. ⁴ Then the king extended the gold scepter to Esther and she arose and stood before him.

⁵ "If it pleases the king," she said, "and if he regards me with favor and thinks it the right thing to do, and if he is pleased with me, let an order be written overruling the dispatches that Haman son of Hammedatha, the Agagite, devised and wrote to destroy the Jews in all the king's provinces. ⁶ For how can I bear to see disaster fall on my people? How can I bear to see the destruction of my family?"

⁷ King Xerxes replied to Queen Esther and to Mordecai the Jew, "Because Haman attacked the Jews, I have given his estate to Esther, and they have impaled him on the pole he set up. ⁸ Now write another decree in the king's name in behalf of the Jews as seems best to you, and seal it with the king's signet ring—for no document written in the king's name and sealed with his ring can be revoked."

Chapter Eight

⁹ At once the royal secretaries were summoned—on the twenty-third day of the third month, the month of Sivan. They wrote out all Mordecai's orders to the Jews, and to the satraps, governors and nobles of the 127 provinces stretching from India to Cush. These orders were written in the script of each province and the language of each people and also to the Jews in their own script and language. ¹⁰ Mordecai wrote in the name of King Xerxes, sealed the dispatches with the king's signet ring, and sent them by mounted couriers, who rode fast horses especially bred for the king.

¹¹ The king's edict granted the Jews in every city the right to assemble and protect themselves; to destroy, kill and annihilate the armed men of any nationality or province who might attack them and their women and children, and to plunder the property of their enemies. ¹² The day appointed for the Jews to do this in all the provinces of King Xerxes was the thirteenth day of the twelfth month, the month of Adar. ¹³ A copy of the text of the edict was to be issued as law in every province and made known to the people of every nationality so that the Jews would be ready on that day to avenge themselves on their enemies.

¹⁴ The couriers, riding the royal horses, went out, spurred on by the king's command, and the edict was issued in the citadel of Susa.

The Triumph of the Jews

¹⁵ When Mordecai left the king's presence, he was wearing royal garments of blue and white, a large crown of gold and a purple robe of fine linen. And the city of Susa held a joyous celebration. ¹⁶ For the Jews it was a time of happiness and joy, gladness and honor. ¹⁷ In every province and in every city to which the edict of the king came, there was joy and gladness among the Jews, with feasting and celebrating. And many people of other nationalities became Jews because fear of the Jews had seized them.

What is the key verse in this chapter?

Chapter Eight

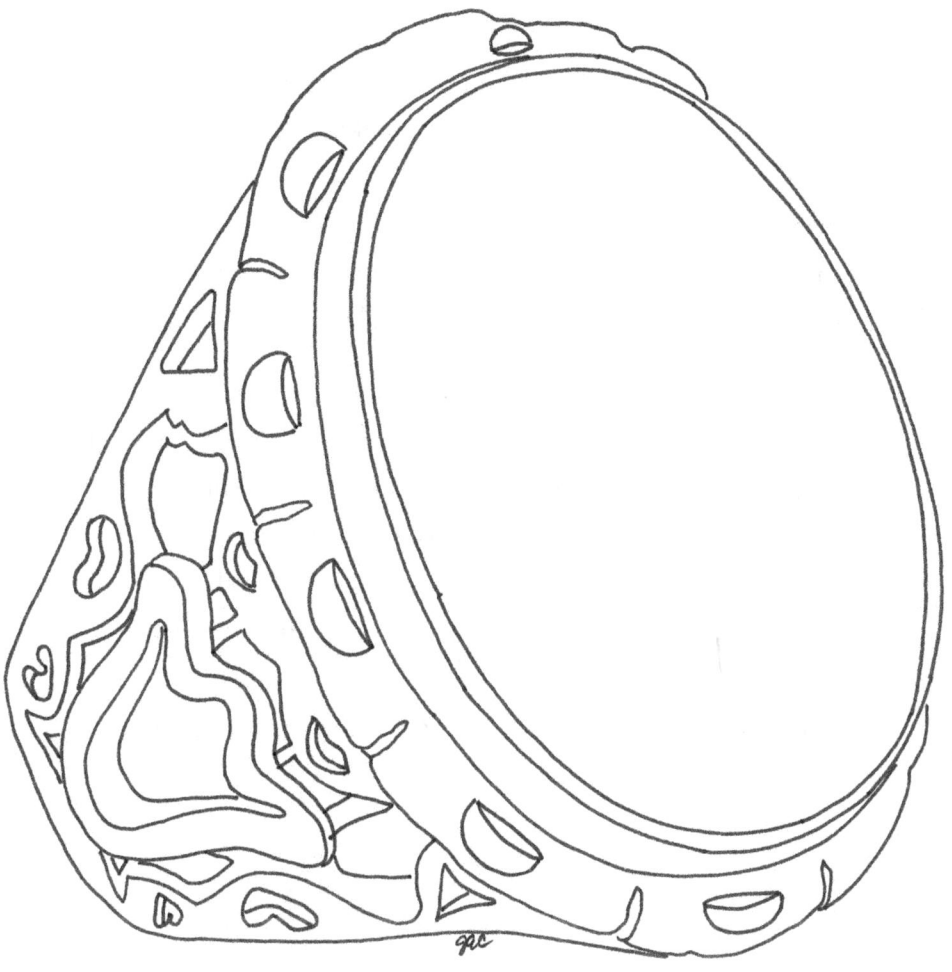

At the end of chapter seven we see that the king's anger was satisfied after he killed Haman for his treachery. He was so grateful to Queen Esther that he gifted the estate of his former advisor to her. He had offered her up to half of his kingdom throughout this book, Here he gives her some of his property. True to form, Esther passes the estate over to her cousin Mordecai. But that still didn't solve the problem. Esther was wisely understood that as long as the edict was out there, her people remained in trouble. As nice as it was to receive the gift of Haman's land, what she really wanted was the safety of her people. Once again, she appealed to her husband to save them, this time openly and emotionally.

The king showed great leadership in this chapter. It is the first time in the book that we see him making a big leadership decision without the help of his cronies. He wasn't enraged, or inebriated. This time we see him calm, rational, and sober. In this moment, he acts like a leader. This new edict was a good strategy not only for him and his kingdom but also saved an entire nation.

Esther's bravery in saving her people from genocide became an official time of celebration. In this chapter we see the very first observance of Purim. In verse 17, we learn that the celebration was infectious. In every city where the edict arrived, people of other nationalities converted, so the Jewish numbers grew.

Has there been a time in your life when circumstances changed dramatically in your favor?

_____

_____

_____

_____

_____

_____

_____

_____

_____

Chapter Eight

How does God show He cares about your problems?

_____
_____
_____
_____
_____
_____
_____
_____

Think about a time when you prayed and you saw your prayers were answered

_____
_____
_____
_____
_____
_____
_____
_____

Have you seen God work in unexpected ways?

___

Take time to pray that God will show you new ways to be used for His glory in your family, with friends and in your community

Please journal your thoughts here

___

Chapter Eight

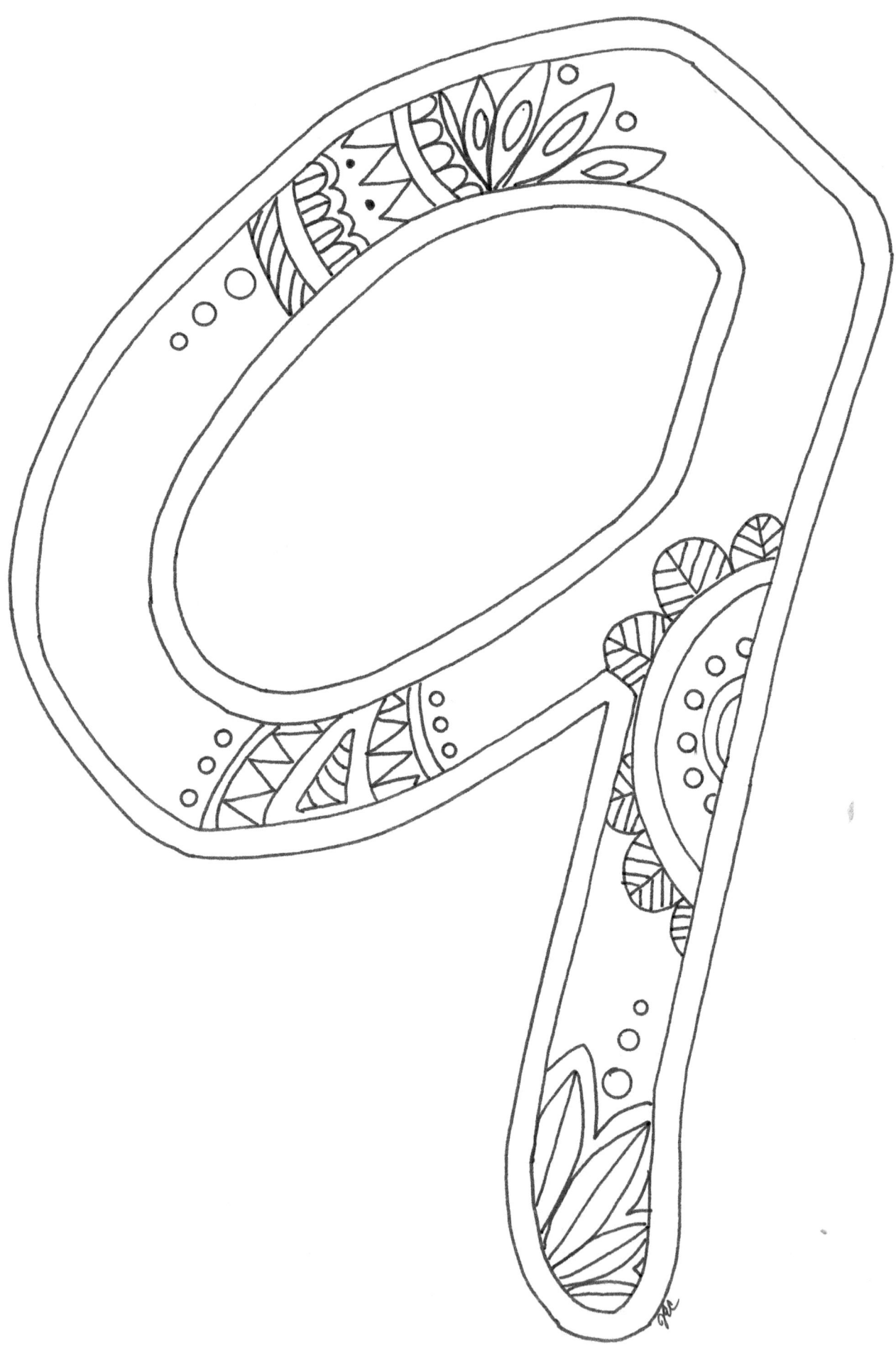

Chapter Nine

¹ On the thirteenth day of the twelfth month, the month of Adar, the edict commanded by the king was to be carried out. On this day the enemies of the Jews had hoped to overpower them, but now the tables were turned and the Jews got the upper hand over those who hated them. ² The Jews assembled in their cities in all the provinces of King Xerxes to attack those determined to destroy them. No one could stand against them, because the people of all the other nationalities were afraid of them. ³ And all the nobles of the provinces, the satraps, the governors and the king's administrators helped the Jews, because fear of Mordecai had seized them. ⁴ Mordecai was prominent in the palace; his reputation spread throughout the provinces, and he became more and more powerful.

⁵ The Jews struck down all their enemies with the sword, killing and destroying them, and they did what they pleased to those who hated them. ⁶ In the citadel of Susa, the Jews killed and destroyed five hundred men. ⁷ They also killed Parshandatha, Dalphon, Aspatha, ⁸ Poratha, Adalia, Aridatha, ⁹ Parmashta, Arisai, Aridai and Vaizatha, ¹⁰ the ten sons of Haman son of Hammedatha, the enemy of the Jews. But they did not lay their hands on the plunder.

¹¹ The number of those killed in the citadel of Susa was reported to the king that same day. ¹² The king said to Queen Esther, "The Jews have killed and destroyed five hundred men and the

ten sons of Haman in the citadel of Susa. What have they done in the rest of the king's provinces? Now what is your petition? It will be given you. What is your request? It will also be granted."

[13] "If it pleases the king," Esther answered, "give the Jews in Susa permission to carry out this day's edict tomorrow also, and let Haman's ten sons be impaled on poles."

[14] So the king commanded that this be done. An edict was issued in Susa, and they impaled the ten sons of Haman. [15] The Jews in Susa came together on the fourteenth day of the month of Adar, and they put to death in Susa three hundred men, but they did not lay their hands on the plunder.

[16] Meanwhile, the remainder of the Jews who were in the king's provinces also assembled to protect themselves and get relief from their enemies. They killed seventy-five thousand of them but did not lay their hands on the plunder. [17] This happened on the thirteenth day of the month of Adar, and on the fourteenth they rested and made it a day of feasting and joy.

[18] The Jews in Susa, however, had assembled on the thirteenth and fourteenth, and then on the fifteenth they rested and made it a day of feasting and joy.

[19] That is why rural Jews—those living in villages—observe the fourteenth of the month of Adar as a day of joy and feasting, a day for giving presents to each other.

Purim Established
[20] Mordecai recorded these events, and he sent letters to all the Jews throughout the provinces of King Xerxes, near and far, [21] to have them celebrate annually the fourteenth and fifteenth days of the month of Adar [22] as the time when the Jews got relief from their enemies, and as the month when their sorrow was

Chapter Nine

turned into joy and their mourning into a day of celebration. He wrote them to observe the days as days of feasting and joy and giving presents of food to one another and gifts to the poor.

²³ So the Jews agreed to continue the celebration they had begun, doing what Mordecai had written to them. ²⁴ For Haman son of Hammedatha, the Agagite, the enemy of all the Jews, had plotted against the Jews to destroy them and had cast the *pur* (that is, the lot) for their ruin and destruction. ²⁵ But when the plot came to the king's attention, he issued written orders that the evil scheme Haman had devised against the Jews should come back onto his own head, and that he and his sons should be impaled on poles. ²⁶ (Therefore these days were called Purim, from the word *pur*.) Because of everything written in this letter and because of what they had seen and what had happened to them, ²⁷ the Jews took it on themselves to establish the custom that they and their descendants and all who join them should without fail observe these two days every year, in the way prescribed and at the time appointed. ²⁸ These days should be remembered and observed in every generation by every family, and in every province and in every city. And these days of Purim should never fail to be celebrated by the Jews—nor should the memory of these days die out among their descendants.

²⁹ So Queen Esther, daughter of Abihail, along with Mordecai the Jew, wrote with full authority to confirm this second letter concerning Purim. ³⁰ And Mordecai sent letters to all the Jews in the 127 provinces of Xerxes' kingdom—words of goodwill and assurance— ³¹ to establish these days of Purim at their designated times, as Mordecai the Jew and Queen Esther had decreed for them, and as they had established for themselves and their descendants in regard to their times of fasting and lamentation. ³² Esther's decree confirmed these regulations

Drawing from the Word

about Purim, and it was written down in the records.

What is the key verse in this chapter?

Esther 9 is all about the feast of Purim for the Jewish people. It took place on the thirteenth, fourteenth and fifteenth day of the twelfth month known as Adar. It is now observed in March.

I spoke with Rabbi Jeff Zameski from a Messianic Temple to get some information about the Feast of Purim. He told me. "The term 'feast of lots' literally translates into Hebrew as *Chag* (feasts of) Purim (lots)." "Lots" refers to the way they made important decisions, much like rolling dice today. It was a common practice at the time. This feast got its name because lots were cast by Haman to determine the day of the genocide, but now they celebrate because God chose that day for salvation. The day had been set aside for destruction and death, instead God used it to save His people.

This day was much more than a regular party though, there was an element of revelry to it. Not only did the edict say that the Jewish people weren't to be killed but it also gave them permission to defend themselves. This must have been a wild idea for a nation of under the rule of another kingdom. They were also given the freedom to pillage the wealth from their oppressors, however Mordecai forbade them from doing so. In fact, this is repeated in verses 15-16 that "they did not lay their hands on the plunder."

It is interesting that Queen Esther is mentioned in verse 29 along with Mordecai as helping to make legislation about the observance of Purim. She didn't sit back and let the men handle things. She had played an instrumental role in all that had happened, and she continued to be a part of it. This is quite a transformation from the timid girl we met in chapter 2, who now creates laws beside the king's advisor.

Sometimes amid our worst times is when God does His greatest works. It's fair to say that nothing went according to anyone's plans in this book. Queen Vashti hadn't expected to be deposed during a party. Esther, as a foreigner, probably never dreamed of becoming queen. Mordecai, who had raised his cousin as his own child plunged into mourning when he heard the news of Haman's plan. The king we met in the beginning was perfectly happy with the way things were going and the advisors that he had. And of course Haman, had chosen to use his power and influence to destroy his enemy. But God changed the course of the story for everyone through His faithful servants. What a wonderful "but God" story this is! Although He isn't implicitly mentioned, we can still see Him at work in the lives of the Jewish people. It was no accident that Mordecai and Esther were put in the palace for such a time as this.

Is there a time in your past when you can see God's hand in changing the course of your plans?

_____

_____

_____

_____

Is there a situation you are currently facing that you need God to intervene in? Perhaps on behalf of someone else

_____

_____

_____

_____

_____

_____

_____

As we can see from throughout this story, God is working for the good of His people. We need to trust Him to do His work in our lives. Is there something that you have been trying to control that you need to give over to God?

_____

_____

_____

_____

_____

_____

Chapter Nine

Why do you think it is hard sometimes to surrender control of a situation, even when we know He is in complete control?

_____

_____

_____

_____

_____

_____

_____

_____

_____

_____

_____

_____

_____

_____

Just like the people of Esther's time, we too can rejoice that God is looking out for us and that He knows the burdens that we bear. What a wonderful reminder of His grace!

Take some time to pray and thank God for a time when he intervened on your, or a loved one's behalf.

Feel free to journal your thoughts here

Chapter Nine

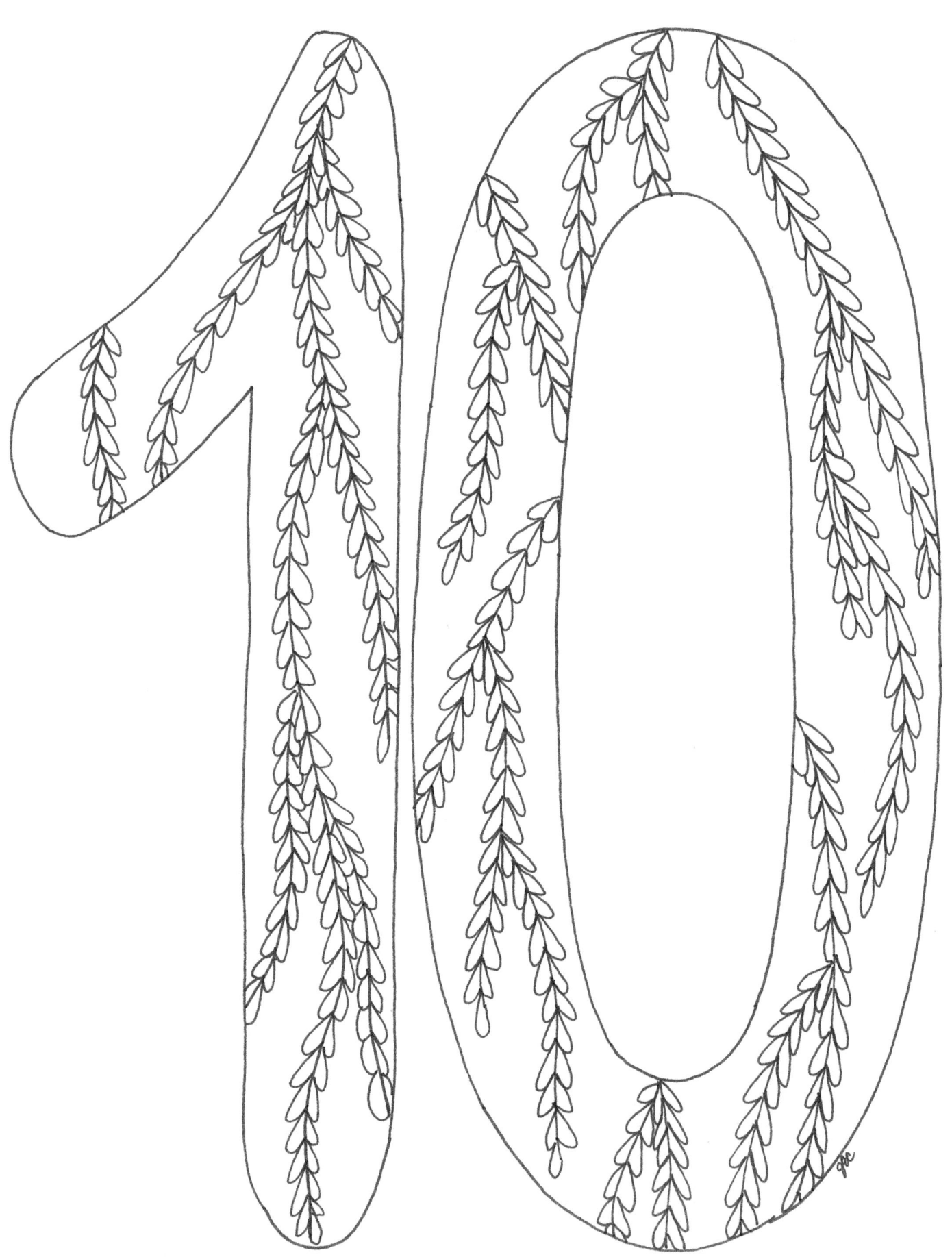

Chapter 10

The Greatness of Mordecai

¹⁰ King Xerxes imposed tribute throughout the empire, to its distant shores. ² And all his acts of power and might, together with a full account of the greatness of Mordecai, whom the king had promoted, are they not written in the book of the annals of the kings of Media and Persia? ³ Mordecai the Jew was second in rank to King Xerxes, preeminent among the Jews, and held in high esteem by his many fellow Jews, because he worked for the good of his people and spoke up for the welfare of all the Jews.

What is the key verse in this passage?

Chapter Ten

We have made it to the end of the exciting book of Esther!

I hope that you have gained some insights along the way. Chapter ten is brief but we can still see a few things happening.

Let's back up a to Esther 8:15: "¹⁵When Mordecai left the king's presence, he was wearing royal garments of blue and white, a large crown of gold and a purple robe of fine linen. And the city of Susa held a joyous celebration."

Mordecai, because of his loyalty to the king traded his sackcloth and ashes to royal garments - even a crown! Then in chapter 9 notice how he was received the king's signet ring and was given permission to send out an edict in the king's name. In this final chapter, we learn that the king wrote about the greatness of his former guard in the official state documents of their history to be remembered forever. He was promoted to second-in-command and made to rule over his own people.

The king had seen something in Mordecai that he hadn't seen in his previous advisors. While they generally were looking out for their own interests, Mordecai was only interested in doing what was right for his people. He also looked after the king. This must have seemed foreign to him. Here was a foreigner with more integrity than all the nobles he'd ever known. Looking at it like that it's easy to see why he held Mordecai in such high esteem.

Chapter Ten

Think about the people you have admired. Do you think that you looked up to them for the right reasons?

_____
_____
_____
_____
_____
_____
_____

Is there someone you know who perhaps deserves more respect from you than you are currently giving them?

_____
_____
_____
_____
_____
_____
_____

Chapter Ten

Identify any areas where you would like to show more integrity like Mordecai.

_____

_____

_____

_____

_____

_____

What are some steps that you can take to work toward becoming a man or women of greater integrity?

_____

_____

_____

_____

_____

_____

Take some time to reflect on what you have gleaned from the story of Esther. Pray as you feel lead.

Drawing from the Word

Journal your thoughts here